WHERE'S MY MONEY?

BY JOHN PATRICK SHANLEY

DRAMATISTS
PLAY SERVICE
INC.

WHERE'S MY MONEY?
Copyright © 2002, John Patrick Shanley

All Rights Reserved

SPECIAL NOTE

SPECIAL NOTE ON SONGS AND RECORDINGS

This play is dedicated to Ira Pittelman, for his humanity.

WHERE'S MY MONEY? was originally produced by the LAByrinth Theater Company (Jinn S. Kim and David Zayas, Producers) in New York City on July 18, 2001. It was directed by John Patrick Shanley; the set design was by Michelle Malavet; the lighting design was by Sarah Sidman; the sound design was by Eric DeArmon; the costume design was by Mimi O'Donnell; and the stage manager was Dawn Wagner. The cast was as follows:

SIDNEY .... David Deblinger
CELESTE .... Yetta Ann Gottesman
HENRY .... John Ortiz (in original production)
Erik Laray Harvey (in subsequent production)
MARCIA MARIE .... Florencia Lozano
TOMMY .... Chris McGarry
NATALIE .... Paula Pizzi

WHERE'S MY MONEY? was subsequently produced by the Manhattan Theatre Club at City Center Stage II (Lynne Meadow, Artistic Director; Barry Grove, Executive Producer) in New York City on November 7, 2001, with the above crew and cast.

CHARACTERS

SIDNEY

CELESTE

HENRY

MARCIA MARIE

TOMMY

NATALIE

SET

Two doors, one tall, one short. Furniture as needed.

WHERE'S MY MONEY?

In the dark is heard the theme music from some whodunit kind of show. We see a series of vignettes, coming attractions, underscored by the music. Each character sees or senses something frightening before the lights cut out.

Lights up on Natalie in a bed, asleep. She starts awake. A nightmare.

Lights bump out on her. Lights up on Sidney, sitting in a chair reading a book. He lowers the book, starts at the sight of something.

Lights out on Sidney. Now we see Marcia Marie. She's in her kitchen with a broom. She turns around, smiling, sees something awful. Lights out.

Henry is discovered, flattened against a wall. The shadow, the hands of someone approaching. Henry cowers in fear.

Blackout. End of vignettes.

Scene 1

Lights up on a French coffee cafe in Soho. We're outside. It's late morning. We see Celeste, a darkly attractive woman with a slightly bohemian feel, talking on a cell phone. She sits at a little blue table, with a hot drink and the remains of a muffin. There's a notebook and paper on the table as well. She has a low voice. She's excited and alarmed by the call.

CELESTE. Wait! She tied knots in his tie, she shoved the tie up his tushie, and then, at the key moment, she ripped the tie out like she was starting a lawn mower. Pup pup pup pup PWONK! The last knot was huge. But here's the twisted part. The next day he goes to the office — he's wearing the tie. Other than that, it wasn't a very good movie. What? What's that? I can't. I can't! I'm in a public place. Turquoise. You are? Right now? You mean for real? I'd like to see that. *(Natalie appears. She's about the same age, also attractive, a little harder maybe, more prosperous. She recognizes Celeste and points and waves. Celeste mimes shock and happiness at seeing Natalie. The following bit of dialogue is overlapped in.)* Natalie! *(She gestures she needs a minute more on the phone, and then says into the receiver.)* Can you hold a second? Shut up! *(Covers the receiver.)* Natalie! How are you? Oh my God!

NATALIE. I'm getting coffee. Should I join you? You have a minute?

CELESTE. Yes! I'll finish up while you're …

NATALIE. Great! *(Natalie goes in. Celeste resumes her call.)*

CELESTE. I gotta go. What about … *(The caller cuts her off.)* What's Friday like for you, Friday night? Kenny's got a gig. Okay, I'll be there. That's just my number. Okay. See ya then. *(She puts her cell away. Natalie returns with coffee.)*

NATALIE. Hey Celeste, whadaya know? It's so great to see you!

CELESTE. You too!

NATALIE. Where did you go?

CELESTE. Where did YOU go? You dropped out of the world! You look great, Natalie. You look really put together.

NATALIE. I sort've am together.

CELESTE. Did I hear you got married?

NATALIE. Two years.

CELESTE. Congratulations!

NATALIE. Thank you. You look so hokie stokie!

CELESTE. What does that mean?

NATALIE. Sex bomb.

CELESTE. I'll accept that.

NATALIE. Are you still with that guy?

CELESTE. Kenny. Yeah.

NATALIE. In the same place?

CELESTE. Yeah, same place. THE ROOM. Where are you?

NATALIE. Upper West Side. Two rooms. It was Henry's aunt's when she ...

CELESTE. What are we doing? Let's sit. I'm set up over here.

NATALIE. Good idea. *(They sit.)* Well. Here we are. The accounting department.

CELESTE. I was secretarial.

NATALIE. Is that a ring on your finger?

CELESTE. I guess so.

NATALIE. I mean it looks like an engagement ring ...

CELESTE. *(Simultaneous.)* An engagement ring.

NATALIE. Well, is it?

CELESTE. That's what Kenny called it.

NATALIE. Well, isn't that what it is then?

CELESTE. He didn't exactly ask me. He just said that's what it was.

NATALIE. A guy says "Here's an engagement ring," it isn't a big leap to ...

CELESTE. Yeah, but he put it on MY Visa card.

NATALIE. Oh. Well that's ...

CELESTE. Questionable. Yeah.

NATALIE. Are you still acting?

CELESTE. I take classes, but I haven't gotten much work. I have a great coach, but my agent is ... I'm not even sure I have an agent. I have to get into that. That's the next thing. There's always a next thing.

NATALIE. But I mean ... did you...?

9

CELESTE. Did I what?

NATALIE. You know. Get an operation?

CELESTE. No, I never did. I decided against it.

NATALIE. So you still have the limp.

CELESTE. Yeah, but it's not very noticeable.

NATALIE. It was the first thing I registered about you. Here was this sexy young girl, she wants to be an actress, but she has a limp. Can they fix it?

CELESTE. There's nothing really wrong to fix. It's how I'm made. It's just a slight disproportion between my left and right hip. I guess, at a certain point, I decided to accept myself as I am.

NATALIE. So if you're not making money acting, how do you get by?

CELESTE. I temp. I'm a secretarial temp. Just like I always was.

NATALIE. Did I hurt your feelings?

CELESTE. No.

NATALIE. I'm such a rhinoceros.

CELESTE. It's better.

NATALIE. Think so?

CELESTE. At least you tell the truth.

NATALIE. That's what I think, but maybe I'm just an asshole.

CELESTE. Even if you are an asshole — which you're not — at least you don't compound it by pretending to be sensitive.

NATALIE. I did hurt your feelings.

CELESTE. Well, what do you think?

NATALIE. So I did. I thought I did.

CELESTE. You just about said I'll never get a job because I'm a cripple.

NATALIE. An acting job.

CELESTE. Well, I'm an actress!

NATALIE. But you don't work.

CELESTE. Lots of actresses don't work!

NATALIE. And maybe those girls shouldn't be actresses.

CELESTE. You got a mouth on you, you know that? I forgot this characteristic. The truthteller.

NATALIE. Well, I'm an accountant. Bottom line.

CELESTE. When it suits you.

NATALIE. What's that mean?

10

CELESTE. Stuff.

NATALIE. Huh?

CELESTE. My white enamel alligator pin.

NATALIE. I don't follow.

CELESTE. You liked it.

NATALIE. What?

CELESTE. When we were working together. I had this white enamel pin. Of an alligator. You liked it, and you did something.

NATALIE. Are we in the same conversation?

CELESTE. I left my jacket over my chair. When I came back from lunch, my white enamel alligator pin was gone.

NATALIE. This is back three years ago?

CELESTE. Yeah.

NATALIE. Are you saying three years ago you thought I took a pin off your jacket while you were at lunch?

CELESTE. It's more like a nagging slight unfounded suspicion I want to definitely put to rest.

NATALIE. There had to be six people in that office, messengers coming and going, the coffee cart. Why would you think it was me?

CELESTE. I don't know.

NATALIE. Did I seem guilty?

CELESTE. No.

NATALIE. Then how did you come to think I took your pin?

CELESTE. No good reason.

NATALIE. But then why did you think it?

CELESTE. *(Big confession.)* Because the day before, I took your red beret!

NATALIE. You did?

CELESTE. Yes.

NATALIE. I had a red beret? I guess I did. You took it?

CELESTE. Yes. I've been carrying that confession around for three years. *(As she removes the beret from her purse.)* Actually, I've been carrying the beret for three years. Here it is back. I'm sorry.

NATALIE. Why would you take this?

CELESTE. Because I'm insane! And then I tried to justify my bad behavior by deciding you took my pin!

NATALIE. But I didn't take your pin!

CELESTE. I know you didn't take it! I wish you had. Then we'd be even. You can just walk away. I'll understand.

NATALIE. Listen. Let's just say we're even, okay? So you took some raggy beret that didn't belong to you. Forgive yourself. We've all done worse.

CELESTE. Thank you.

NATALIE. No big deal.

CELESTE. I'm such a case.

NATALIE. Forget it.

CELESTE. No. You're a nicer person than me.

NATALIE. No I'm not.

CELESTE. Yes, you are. I wanna learn from you. I wanna learn to deal. Maybe I should look at my life without makeup. My life is bad. Well, it's not that bad but ... I enjoy reading. I don't wanna feel sorry for myself but ...

NATALIE. Is it Kenny?

CELESTE. He's not helping. But it's him too. I'm not getting work and I'm turning thirty, and I just got this huge bill for the ring ...

NATALIE. I would've thought you'd already turned thirty?

CELESTE. ALL RIGHT, I've TURNED thirty! So your marriage is good?

NATALIE. I mean, actually, you must be thirty-one.

CELESTE. Yes. All right. I forgot. You ARE an accountant. Thirty-one. I'm glad we got that straightened out. So how's your marriage? Good? Better? Bad?

NATALIE. It's good.

CELESTE. Nice for you. I'm glad. And you have a job you like?

NATALIE. It's solid.

CELESTE. So you see what you're saying? Look at the picture. You've got a life.

NATALIE. Well, I made choices.

CELESTE. (She cries.) No. It's karma. I try to make choices, but nothing sticks. I just float.

NATALIE. How's Kenny doing?

CELESTE. I think Kenny hates me.

NATALIE. He does not!

CELESTE. We've been together for so long, and his life is so not happening, and he is smoking so much dope.

12

NATALIE. How's the band?

CELESTE. The band broke up. Kenny does weddings now as a pickup deal. But mostly he just sits in the apartment and looks at me like I'm "The Thing That Ate His Life."

NATALIE. Is he depressed?

CELESTE. He's a lazy, stoned drummer in a cheap Hawaiian shirt. He's like a depressing piece of furniture. What's your husband do?

NATALIE. He's a lawyer.

CELESTE. A lawyer. What happened to that other guy?

NATALIE. Who?

CELESTE. You know who.

NATALIE. Tommy. Well, I knew that wasn't going to work out. That was just sex.

CELESTE. You were nuts about him.

NATALIE. He was a porter. I wasn't going to marry a porter.

CELESTE. Did he ask you?

NATALIE. No.

CELESTE. That was hot. That thing you had with him.

NATALIE. You never saw us.

CELESTE. I remember the way you looked. He was all over the way you looked.

NATALIE. Yeah, well, it was hot.

CELESTE. I feel like running something by you.

NATALIE. What?

CELESTE. Maybe not.

NATALIE. All right.

CELESTE. I'm having an affair.

NATALIE. Oh wow. Who?

CELESTE. Six months now.

NATALIE. Does Kenny know?

CELESTE. He acts like he doesn't but, I mean ... There's evidence.

NATALIE. Phone calls?

CELESTE. No. Bruises.

NATALIE. So this guy's violent?

CELESTE. WE'RE violent. We both have a lot of anger. It's sort've Latin.

NATALIE. He's Latin?

CELESTE. No.

13

NATALIE. Uh-huh. So you hit him, too?

CELESTE. No. But we're in it together. It must sound bad. It's hard to explain.

NATALIE. Why'd you tell me?

CELESTE. I haven't told anybody.

NATALIE. Then why me?

CELESTE. He slaps me. He spanks me. He makes me crawl around the floor like a dog. He calls me names. And then I go home to Kenny and act like nothing happened.

NATALIE. So Kenny knows.

CELESTE. I don't know. Kenny blows so much weed he may think I'm something on TV.

NATALIE. He must know.

CELESTE. Who knows what Kenny knows? He's English.

NATALIE. And this guy you're having this …

CELESTE. He has read the book that God wrote on my flesh. I've always been afraid to say what I want. He knows what I want and he makes me do it. Get this. He gave me a gun.

NATALIE. He what?

CELESTE. Sometimes I'd be headed home late. He was worried about me. So he gave me a little gun. How sexy is that? I know. Sick.

NATALIE. Not necessarily. But what's the deal exactly?

CELESTE. There is no deal. I see him about once every week and a half. He calls me, I show up somewhere, and he burns down my fucking house.

NATALIE. He's married.

CELESTE. Yeah. I don't care.

NATALIE. You care.

CELESTE. You know what I mean.

NATALIE. And you know what I mean.

CELESTE. Let me control the way I tell this story, okay?

NATALIE. Okay.

CELESTE. There's an atmosphere with this guy … of murder. He wouldn't murder me — that's not what I'm saying — but it's there. Like an aroma. I could smell this thing on him when we met. He was introducin' himself, sayin' hello, bein' nice. We're in a public place. I remember thinkin', he's going to rape me. And seeing like, police photographs in my head. Of me. And right like that, right out of that, I gave him my phone number. I walked away like there was a camera recording me and music I was walking to. And I felt like I was in a ghost story about love. A week later, we meet up. I'm alone with him for the first time. It's in his office. I walk in his office. He closes the door. "Click." And I feel this weight come over my arms and legs. I was scared. 'Cause he was goin' to do something to me. And I wanted him to do something to me. I was afraid and I wanted to be afraid. I wanted fear. I was tired of being "good girl." The first time I went to him, I went to his office. I dressed all in white. Can you imagine? Like a sacrifice. I had this book, *Return of the Native*. And I just started talking about Eustacia Vye because I was so nervous. And he didn't call me on it. He didn't say, "What are you talking about this book? That's not what's going on here." He just talked back to me about Eustacia Vye. But while he talked, he put his hand on the bone in my chest, and he slowly pushed me down. He never stopped talking about what I was talking about, but he was pushing and I was going down. And then his hands and my whole anatomy went to this other world and we did things without words. What we were saying was like we were one bunch of people in one room, but what we were doing was we were another bunch of people in a very different room. A room without words. We had a secret from ourselves. There was a lot of blood. I got my period right in the middle … He's … He was big. I guess it knocked something loose. He hadda go out to a store and buy me a raincoat to put over myself. 'Cause, Natalie, I looked like I'd just been born. And this was in an office. This was in a man's office. In the middle of the day. Do you know what I'm talking about? You do kinda, don't you?

NATALIE. Celeste.

CELESTE. What?

NATALIE. I don't like this whole freaking thing! What are you doing?

CELESTE. I know.

NATALIE. I don't see you for two years …

CELESTE. But you do know what I'm talking about, don't you? In some way?

NATALIE. No.

CELESTE. God, I really thought in some way you would … I

haven't told anyone. I thought you …

NATALIE. You were mistaken.

CELESTE. I guess we never knew each other very well.

NATALIE. No.

CELESTE. But you were more like me … before.

NATALIE. Maybe. Maybe I was turned on by dangerous, stupid shit when I was younger.

CELESTE. Okay. I'd appreciate it if you didn't … repeat this conversation.

NATALIE. I won't.

CELESTE. But I am little bummed out that we can't talk. I need to talk to somebody. I can be pretty hard on myself.

NATALIE. I think you're inviting a conversation you don't wanna have.

CELESTE. But I do want to have it. Look, I'm in trouble.

NATALIE. You're in some underworld.

CELESTE. Yes, I am. That's true.

NATALIE. But you wanna see it as positive and I can't help you with that. It's not positive. You've got it wrong.

CELESTE. Then straighten me out.

NATALIE. Are you sure?

CELESTE. Yeah. I'm inviting it. I want a reaction.

NATALIE. All right, I'll just lay it out for you. You're a whore.

CELESTE. What?!

NATALIE. Don't. Please. It's hard enough without you playing surprised. Don't tell me you haven't thought about the fact that you're a whore. A STUPID whore.

CELESTE. Natalie.

NATALIE. I'll break it down for you. First thing. The count. Let's do the count. You're thirty-one. Next year, you'll be guess what? Twenty-three? No. Thirty-two. And it goes on from there. Older, older, older. A flight of stairs going down, down, down. You're like a quart of milk reaching its expiration date. Have you ever tried to sell a pumpkin the day after Halloween? That's what you are facing. Are you ready? I don't think so. Is it just? Who cares. Pick a fight with God. See where you get. It's the truth of what it is to be a woman.

CELESTE. Not in France.

16

NATALIE. France! Then go to France! Climb the Eiffel Tower. Feed the pigeons. Maybe they'll be glad to see you. Please! You're in America. Do the math. Next. You've gotta face the facts. You've got a birth defect. You've got a limp. How many parts are there for limping girls?

CELESTE. Laura in *The Glass Menagerie*.

NATALIE. *(Simultaneous.)* Laura in *The Glass Menagerie*. And that's it! Have there been any productions of that play?

CELESTE. Yes.

NATALIE. And did you get that part?

CELESTE. No.

NATALIE. Then it's time for you to stop office-temping and doing Romeo's girlfriend in acting class and get a bona-fide fucking job. It's two plus two. You have to drop the lollipop and pick up the car keys! Next issue. Kenny. This may sound tough, but I'm going to say it anyway. Kenny's your best bet.

CELESTE. No way!

NATALIE. Yes, he's a loser. But what are you at this point? Maybe together you can pull your car out of the ditch and make some miles down the road. I know where you're at, Celeste. There's a million women like you. You don't want to look at your story 'cause you don't like your story, so you just close your eyes and tell yourself a fucking fairy tale. And you know what that makes you? In a world of men? Totally exploitable. 'Cause you want the lie. You got no interest in the truth. What's the truth ever done for you? The truth of your life is like a bad magazine. Boring story, lousy pictures. Which brings me to your mysterious, exciting, cheeseball stud. Who smacks you around because he's afraid of his wife. Do I even have to talk about this rodent? A married violent scumbug who slips you a Saturday Night Special for what? Valentines Day? You can't look at what this guy pegged the minute he smelled that thriftshop essential oil you use for perfume. You're a pushover. Is this your notebook?

CELESTE. You don't like my oil?

NATALIE. What have you been writing?

CELESTE. Poetry.

NATALIE. Poetry. You're going down in flames. Unless you get it together, they are going to pass you around like chicken wings.

CELESTE. I can't believe you called me a whore.

NATALIE. Hasn't he called you a whore? Haven't you called yourself a whore?

CELESTE. Never mind what I call myself! We're talking about you.

NATALIE. No, we're talking about you. I'm not the one in trouble. What's your definition of a whore anyway?

CELESTE. I don't know.

NATALIE. A romantic woman. Romance is for men. Women who settle for romance get used.

CELESTE. Where do you get off? What is this conversation?

NATALIE. This is the conversation you wanted.

CELESTE. Well, I'm stopping it!

NATALIE. Suit yourself.

CELESTE. You have no right to call me what you called me.

NATALIE. I have the right.

CELESTE. How do you figure that?

NATALIE. Because I was a whore, too. A sloppy, stupid whore. But then I made a choice.

CELESTE. To what?

NATALIE. Not be. There are two groups of women in the world. You've got a choice to make.

CELESTE. What about following your soul?

NATALIE. What if you have a damned soul? Are you gonna follow it down to the burning shitheaps of hell?

CELESTE. Maybe.

NATALIE. You are ten years old. You don't get it, do you? How about this. I wouldn't even introduce you to my husband. How about that?

CELESTE. Why not?

NATALIE. What if your soul told you to fuck him?

CELESTE. That's ridiculous.

NATALIE. It's not ridiculous. You probably would fuck him.

CELESTE. I would not! What do you think I am?

NATALIE. I already told you what I think you are. And what every woman like me thinks every woman like you would do if she got the chance.

CELESTE. But off what basis do you say such a thing?

NATALIE. You like it to be wrong. To be a secret. A married man

18

is the perfect thing.

CELESTE. You have no romantic feelings!

NATALIE. What I have and what I do are two separate things.

CELESTE. You said you were a whore.

NATALIE. And I was.

CELESTE. So were you with a married man?

NATALIE. No. But it was bad anyway.

CELESTE. How?

NATALIE. He wasn't a serious contestant. He was uneducated, he had a dead-end job, health problems. He was rough with me. My feelings about him were cheap.

CELESTE. Romantic.

NATALIE. Same thing.

CELESTE. Maybe you're the one who needs to be straightened out.

NATALIE. I don't think so.

CELESTE. All right. Look. I know you have a point, but the only thing that makes me get up in the morning is this guy. Everything else is lousy. I have to have something to look forward to.

NATALIE. Give him up. Marry Kenny.

CELESTE. Aren't you afraid to give such big advice? I mean, what if you're wrong?

NATALIE. I'm not wrong.

CELESTE. What if what was right for you isn't right for me? We're very different people.

NATALIE. We're different because I got on with my life, and you didn't.

CELESTE. What if we're more different than that?

NATALIE. Everybody's basically the same. I was you.

CELESTE. I don't believe that.

NATALIE. That's because you're a romantic. There is no one right person for you, Celeste. This isn't about destiny. It's about making decisions with your head instead of your ass.

CELESTE. But what about my needs?

NATALIE. You need a roof over your head. You need an orthopedic surgeon.

CELESTE. I need other things more than that. And if I don't get those things, I don't get being alive.

NATALIE. Enough. Bite the bullet, make the changes.

CELESTE. You're tougher than me.

NATALIE. That's an alibi. But even if it's true, you can get tougher.

CELESTE. I'm frightened to do that.

NATALIE. I thought you liked being frightened?

CELESTE. I don't wanna live an idea instead of a life.

NATALIE. Are you saying that's what I'm doing?

CELESTE. You tell me.

NATALIE. All right, that's exactly what I'm doing. I'm controlling what happens in my life. I'm looking down on my day and moving stuff around till it's right. I'm in control.

CELESTE. I went to a self-actualizing kinesiologist yesterday.

NATALIE. What is that?

CELESTE. Sort of a psychic.

NATALIE. Oh God. That is so perfect.

CELESTE. She told me I was going to see my future today.

NATALIE. Maybe I'm the future you.

CELESTE. I don't want to be you.

NATALIE. Celeste. You're pathetic. Wake up! Would you? It's sad to watch somebody just fuck everything up. I think you need to go home, take a good hard look in the mirror, get real, make choices. You need to take one day and get brutally realistic about the facts of your life. And DO something about it.

CELESTE. You don't know the things I think about. When I'm alone. It's okay, I know what to do. *(A man, Tommy, appears and approaches their table. Celeste sees him first.)* Hello?

TOMMY. Hello. *(Natalie turns and sees the man. She almost faints. Celeste doesn't know what's going on.)*

CELESTE. Is there ... ? Natalie? Natalie? *(But Natalie only stares at the man.)*

TOMMY. Where's my money? Where's my money, Natalie?

CELESTE. Is he b...? *(To the man:)* Excuse me. Excuse me? Shoo! Come on! Back to weird world! Schmuck. *(The man just walks off slowly.)* Who was that? *(No answer.)* Are you okay? Should I ... I'll get you some water. *(Natalie grabs Celeste as she gets up, stopping her. She's frightened.)*

NATALIE. Stay!

20

CELESTE. What is it? Are you in trouble?
NATALIE. No.
CELESTE. Do you owe that man money?
NATALIE. Yes.
CELESTE. How much do you owe him?
NATALIE. A couple of thousand dollars. Twenty-seven hundred dollars.
CELESTE. And you haven't got it?
NATALIE. You don't understand.
CELESTE. Is he a criminal? Are you ... *(In danger?)*
NATALIE. He's ...
CELESTE. 'Cause I could walk you right over to the police station.
NATALIE. That man's been dead for two years. *(Blackout. A pronounced wolf howl is heard as Natalie and Celeste look at each other. Something like Howlin' Wolf singing "I Asked for Water" kicks in as we move to the apartment.* *)*

Scene 2

A working class bedroom on the Upper West Side. Music is playing on a boom box. The music is something like Howlin' Wolf singing "I Asked For Water"; it's pretty loud. *Discovered: Henry and Natalie. He's about twenty-seven, a self-educated street guy reading a book in his bathrobe.*

Natalie's in a brightly colored T-shirt and a man's boxers. She regards him a moment. Then she starts dancing to the music, seductive. No response from Henry. He looks at her and goes back to reading. Suddenly, she barks.

NATALIE. Henry! I'm in the room. Can you deal with the music please?
HENRY. *(He hits the button on the player to stop the music.)* Yes,

* See Special Note on Songs and Recordings on copyright page.

my precious little co-habitator?

NATALIE. How can you read and listen to that voodoo music?

HENRY. I like to do two things at once. I'm like you that way.

NATALIE. What's the book?

HENRY. *Crime and Punishment.*

NATALIE. Why do you like that?

HENRY. Who said I like it?

NATALIE. Why would you read something you don't like?

HENRY. Who said I don't like it?

NATALIE. You're such a fuckin' lawyer.

HENRY. I'm reading about guilt. Not guilt in court. Guilt inside. Most things never get to court. Most trials go on in the heart. This is the minutes of a trial conducted in the heart. Sidney was reading it. He lent it to me.

NATALIE. You wanna be like Sidney.

HENRY. No, I do not. I wanna BE Sidney. He's a partner. And he didn't pass the bar the first time.

NATALIE. Neither did you.

HENRY. That's my point. It shows that it doesn't mean shit about ultimately achieving my desire. Sidney did it. I'll do it. Simple as that.

NATALIE. You will.

HENRY. That's right. I will. Because I never give up. Even if I should.

NATALIE. I count on that.

HENRY. Yeah. You left the front door open again.

NATALIE. You're such a nudge.

HENRY. And when I went to play my music, there was music in there I've never heard. You have secret music?

NATALIE. Listen, why don't we get a joint checking account?

HENRY. We've been through that.

NATALIE. I know. Your first wife fucked you over so now you handle the money.

HENRY. Left me nothin' but a King Tut medal.

NATALIE. But you wear it.

HENRY. What, are you jealous of King Tut?

NATALIE. It's a bit of her.

HENRY. That bug you?

NATALIE. Yeah.

HENRY. You never said.

NATALIE. I said it now.

HENRY. Fair enough. Point taken. *(He removes the medal from his neck and gives it to her.)* Here.

NATALIE. Just like that?

HENRY. Just like that. Problem solved. Life as it should be.

NATALIE. All right. Hasta la vista, golden boy. Back to Cairo. *(She tosses the medal; to Henry.)* You the man.

HENRY. Just steppin' up. Give you a role model.

NATALIE. I don't need a role model.

HENRY. You kiddin'?! Have I ever said no to you?

NATALIE. No.

HENRY. You need money?

NATALIE. No.

HENRY. Those my boxers?

NATALIE. Yeah.

HENRY. Fuckin' thief. Why don't they look like that on me?

NATALIE. That's where I come in.

HENRY. *(Re: a pin on the boxer shorts.)* What's that?

NATALIE. Just a pin to hold them up.

HENRY. A little alligator. *(He steps away, examining her.)* Is that you?

NATALIE. Very nice.

HENRY. But there's a thing I can't figure for Sidney. His wife. What's that about?

NATALIE. I'm the accountant. I should be the one doing the numbers.

HENRY. History says otherwise. There's a little matter of a two hundred dollar fork.

NATALIE. That was handmade, solid silver.

HENRY. Silver costs something like six dollars an ounce. The fork weighed about two ounces. That brings us up to twelve dollars. The other hundred and eighty-eight was for what?

NATALIE. Workmanship.

HENRY. Workmanship my long-suffering ass. How about the one hundred and ten dollar candle?

NATALIE. That was a very beautiful thing!

HENRY. It was, but then you lit it. And it melted like candles do. You are not going to eat through our savings buying the crazy

23

things you like to buy. Now, I'd like to discuss this book. The issue in this story is how long can this guilty motherfucker live with it? That's the question. Everything else is known. The crime and who did it is known. Everything except the exact weight of hypocrisy a man can't carry. And that question is what makes me turn the page. Who woulda thought that was such an interesting question to me? Life ain't like that, is it?

NATALIE. Like what?

HENRY. Life doesn't have that narrative drive. Life doesn't hook you.

NATALIE. Sometimes it does.

HENRY. No, life is boring. People are boring. Books and movies are fake because fake is better. In books and movies the story syncopates. It finishes with a bang. Life is a siege. Life is an army outside a city that never falls. I have clients come in and tell me their story and it's always the same fuckin' cha-cha. They blame somebody. Everybody comes in and blames the other one. He did this, she did that. Playin' the blame game. People are predictable as Monday after Sunday and boring as a bag lunch.

NATALIE. Am I boring?

HENRY. Absolutely.

NATALIE. Bite me.

HENRY. As a story. What's the big revelation with you? Nothing. You're an ordinary person.

NATALIE. Maybe you're just failing to see how interesting I am?

HENRY. No, I'm not.

NATALIE. Maybe I'm boring to you ...

HENRY. As a STORY.

NATALIE. ... 'cause you're boring and your understanding of people is boring.

HENRY. If something interesting were to manifest, trust me pumpkin, I would be goosed. I'm on a vigil for that shit.

NATALIE. No. You keep things boring because that's how you like it.

HENRY. Okay. And how do I do that?

NATALIE. Like with the checking account. You're afraid to be surprised by what I'd do if it was a joint account.

HENRY. You mean I don't want the excitement of getting ripped off?

24

NATALIE. I wouldn't rip you off.

HENRY. Of course you wouldn't 'cause you can't.

NATALIE. Goddammit, I'm not some hustler trying to get over on you, Henry! I'm your fucking wife!

HENRY. Oh, you're flashin' the credential. The wife.

NATALIE. Damn right I am!

HENRY. So we're gettin' serious.

NATALIE. I am exactly serious. I've been serious.

HENRY. That's grim.

NATALIE. We're married married married, when does the trust kick in? When are you gonna relax with me and take the ride?

HENRY. Why do you want a joint checking account?

NATALIE. So I can write checks.

HENRY. You tell me the check, I'll write it.

NATALIE. I wanna write the check!

HENRY. What check?

NATALIE. No check in particular. If you died, I'd get the money!

HENRY. So you're fantasizing my death.

NATALIE. If we divorce, I'm entitled.

HENRY. Oh, you want a divorce. All right. 70/30 and you're out.

NATALIE. You are so into intimidation.

HENRY. I'm a matrimonial lawyer. That's the job.

NATALIE. You're my husband, that's the job.

HENRY. I don't think that's supposed to be a job.

NATALIE. With me? Are you serious? I'm twenty-five hours a day, eight days a week. I'm the hardest job in — *(He kisses her.)* America.

HENRY. That's my job.

NATALIE. I don't want a divorce.

HENRY. Why not?

NATALIE. Too expensive.

HENRY. Sport of kings.

NATALIE. Divorce.

HENRY. You were the first one to use the word.

NATALIE. Take it back.

HENRY. Is that allowed?

NATALIE. Make it up to you.

HENRY. How?

25

NATALIE. Whatever you want.

HENRY. How 'bout love?

NATALIE. That's what I want, too. I don't want to be married by myself.

HENRY. Me neither.

NATALIE. I know.

HENRY. But how do I get you?

NATALIE. I'm right here.

HENRY. Me too.

NATALIE. What's in the way?

HENRY. Us.

NATALIE. Henry, let's do it. Tell me what to do.

HENRY. Tell me what you want.

NATALIE. I need you to tell me what to do.

HENRY. What do you want to do?

NATALIE. Just tell me and I'll do it. Anything.

HENRY. What?

NATALIE. Jesus! You're killing the whole thing!

HENRY. Why didn't you tell me?

NATALIE. Why don't you know?

HENRY. Don't bother with me then! I was readin' my book, listenin' to my music!

NATALIE. Sucking your fucking thumb.

HENRY. That shitass attitude.

NATALIE. It's just the truth.

HENRY. Then I don't want the truth.

NATALIE. Then talk to somebody else.

HENRY. No! You! I'm talkin' to you. You think you're smarter than me.

NATALIE. No, I don't, Henry.

HENRY. Well, you're not! "I can do the checkin' account!" If you're so smart, why don't you have a checkin' account I wanna be joint with? Huh? I'll tell you why. 'Cause I'm the thing that makes this marriage work. Not you!

NATALIE. Okay.

HENRY. I've always been the thing! That's why you married me. Because I could make it happen for you. You would've just ... had no life without me. No stability. I give you the check when you need the check. You can depend on that. It's boring how you can depend I'll be there every day. Not walk out. Show up with the money. You're right. I'm the one makes this marriage boring. But you're the one who needs for it to be boring. Because you, if you were left to your tricks, you would destroy the world. That's who you are.

NATALIE. The world? Would that include, like, Australia?

HENRY. You know what I'm talking about.

NATALIE. What do you want from me?

HENRY. Nothing.

NATALIE. I'm sorry.

HENRY. I can't want anything from you. And why not? You got no money left from your pay?

NATALIE. I'm still catching up the credit cards.

HENRY. Good luck. Now why do you want a joint checking account?

NATALIE. I just thought it would show respect.

HENRY. Don't waste my fucking time! Why do you want a joint checking account? *(She starts crying.)* What's this?

NATALIE. I'm scared.

HENRY. That I believe. Why?

NATALIE. I don't wanna say.

HENRY. Why not?

NATALIE. You'll judge me.

HENRY. Fuck that. I hate judges. That's not what I do. I'm an adversarial man. I've got a point of view and I take sides! Now why are you scared?

NATALIE. I saw something that couldn't be.

HENRY. Good for you.

NATALIE. You don't understand.

HENRY. Fine. You'll explain it to me.

NATALIE. I saw a ghost! Okay? I saw a ghost.

HENRY. What ghost? Whose ghost?

NATALIE. Tommy.

HENRY. *(A pause.)* Where?

NATALIE. A coffee place. Middle of the day. I was with a friend. She saw him, too.

HENRY. A ghost.

27

NATALIE. Yes.

HENRY. Well, how 'bout that.

NATALIE. I know.

HENRY. That is some first-class stamp. That is a level of validation I didn't think I would ever get.

NATALIE. I guess it is.

HENRY. Say something to me.

NATALIE. I'm sorry.

HENRY. For what?

NATALIE. For not believing you when you told me you saw a ghost.

HENRY. You laughed in my face.

NATALIE. Well, of course I did. It seemed so ...

HENRY. Crazy. I know. We're married, married, married. When's the trust kick in? When I see a ghost or when you see one?

NATALIE. All right. You've got a point.

HENRY. My mother came back.

NATALIE. All right, I believe you.

HENRY. It was the biggest moment in my life. It's the reason I'm not a junkie today. And you laughed in my face.

NATALIE. Well I'm sorry.

HENRY. She came right through the wall, busted my stereo all to shit! She had a number eight frying pan in her right hand. She said, "You stick that needle in your arm again, sonny boy, and I'll take your head off the payroll!" Looked me in the eye. It was love. It was love made her come back and save me. What made Tommy come back? Was it love?

NATALIE. Money.

HENRY. *(He starts laughing.)* Money? What's Tommy gonna do with money? He's dead!

NATALIE. I owe him twenty-seven hundred dollars.

HENRY. That's a very specific amount.

NATALIE. I borrowed it from him.

HENRY. When? What for?

NATALIE. I bought my wedding dress with it.

HENRY. *(This stops Henry.)* I thought your father bought you that? *(Natalie shakes her head.)* You went to Tommy? Why would you go to Tommy? Why didn't you come to me?

28

NATALIE. Oh Henry, you were in the middle of struggling yourself.

HENRY. You were through with Tommy! You broke his heart! Why would you ask him for money?

NATALIE. He had it.

HENRY. He didn't have it anymore than I did. He was a janitor. He didn't even have clean clothes. Why him and not me?

NATALIE. I can't piece it together now. It made sense at the time.

HENRY. I knew there was something.

NATALIE. I didn't even know I was gonna do it, I just did it.

HENRY. There's always been something. A missing piece.

NATALIE. This has nothing to do with us.

HENRY. This has everything to do with us!

NATALIE. No, this was before. This was Tommy. I just wanted revenge.

HENRY. Revenge for what? You left him!

NATALIE. I thought I was going to talk to him, but then I got mad at him and I asked him for money to look good for you. Twenty-seven hundred dollars. It was all the money he had. And he gave it to me. I thought he wouldn't. That's why I asked for it. I thought that would be the break. But then he gave it to me.

HENRY. Did you fuck him?

NATALIE. Yes. It was before we were married.

HENRY. *(He grabs his clothes.)* I'm not sleeping here tonight.

NATALIE. Don't leave me alone.

HENRY. Why not?

NATALIE. I'm scared.

HENRY. You know why you're scared?

NATALIE. He didn't love me.

HENRY. Did you love him?

NATALIE. No.

HENRY. That's fucked up.

NATALIE. He treated me like an animal! He called me a whore! Every time! Like I was nothing!

HENRY. Then why'd you keep going back?

NATALIE. He had a hold on me.

HENRY. He still does.

NATALIE. He's dead!

29

HENRY. So what! You still want something from him.

NATALIE. He degraded me and I wanted back at him!

HENRY. To an endless point?

NATALIE. To the fucking grave.

HENRY. Looks like you didn't stop there. Looks like you dug him up.

NATALIE. Where you gonna sleep?

HENRY. Who said I'm gonna sleep?

NATALIE. Look! There's no need to go. This thing ... It's the past!

HENRY. The past is real.

NATALIE. Where you going?

HENRY. Out to the world, my love.

NATALIE. What if he comes again? I don't want to be alone. *(Henry's dressed.)*

HENRY. Hey, you're never alone. We just found that out. You sit here, you wait. Maybe I'll be back. Now here's a story come alive, right? What's gonna happen next? Let's turn the page. *(He exits. She cries. She stops. She reaches under the bed, grabs a small box, takes out a joint, and lights it. She takes a couple of hits. She goes over to the CD player, picks up a loose CD, and puts it on the boom box. Turns off the light. Streetlight floods the room. Music starts to play, maybe Marcia Ball singing "Another Man's Woman."* She takes another hit on the joint. The man, the ghost, Tommy, appears backlit in the doorway. She sees him. She is not surprised. Slowly, she gets up, goes to him. He meets her halfway. They begin to dance. Dreamy. Dreamy. Then he begins to strangle her. She tries to scream, can't. He roars at her.)*

TOMMY. Where's my money, Natalie?! Where is it?! Where?! *(Blackout. Simultaneous music out. She screams. Lights up. Daytime. Natalie's in bed, awakening from a nightmare. She starts sobbing.)*

NATALIE. Oh Tommy! Tommy! *(The lights fade. Music. Something like Irma Thomas singing "Time is on My Side" begins to play.* The lights fade ever so slowly.)*

Scene 3

A scuffed, green metal desk, dirty venetian blinds, a couple of chairs. A middle-aged guy in a cheap suit, Sidney, sits behind the desk reading a book, chewing gum. A knock.

SIDNEY. Come in. *(Henry comes in. His clothes are wrinkled. He hasn't bathed.)* Henry.

HENRY. Ay, Sidney. Busy?

SIDNEY. As it's you, no. *(He hears something.)* Did you hear that?

HENRY. What?

SIDNEY. Nothing. The goddamn hot water in this building, it's a presence. Come on, sit down.

HENRY. Thanks. Always with the book. What are you readin' now?

SIDNEY. *Casanova.*

HENRY. The lover.

SIDNEY. That's right. How are you doing with the *Crime and Punishment?*

HENRY. I'm marching through it. Sometimes it's good.

SIDNEY. It falls apart at the end. He goes to jail, his brain collapses, and he finds God. You're a little disheveled.

HENRY. A bit. *(Indicating the book.)* So you're interested in love?

SIDNEY. Oh yeah.

HENRY. What do you think of a guy like that? So many women?

SIDNEY. Good for him. He was a true believer. And when he finally became cynical, which took him a long time to do, he didn't become cynical about the women. He became cynical about himself. *(He hears something again.)* What IS that sound?

HENRY. I don't hear anything.

SIDNEY. You're lucky. It's a curse to be sensitive.

HENRY. How do you know if you've become cynical about yourself?

SIDNEY. I think it starts when you begin to notice your own innocence.

31

HENRY. Have you had that experience?

SIDNEY. Never.

HENRY. You're not so tough.

SIDNEY. Please yourself. I love being underestimated.

HENRY. Are you superstitious?

SIDNEY. I won't walk under a ladder, but that's about the extent.

HENRY. I may not be able to tell you this story then.

SIDNEY. You're not baiting me, are you?

HENRY. No, no. I'm a little tired.

SIDNEY. Marital trouble?

HENRY. How'd you know?

SIDNEY. I'm a divorce lawyer. *(The phone rings. Sidney picks it up.)* Yeah? Hold my calls. I'm with a potential client. *(He hangs up the phone.)* Talk to me.

HENRY. Wait a minute.

SIDNEY. What she do?

HENRY. I'm not getting divorced.

SIDNEY. You're right. Let's stay away from the result. Let's look at the cause of your anguish.

HENRY. I guess that's the important thing. The core issue. Unfaithful, Sidney. She was unfaithful to me.

SIDNEY. Can you prove it?

HENRY. I don't need to.

SIDNEY. In this state you do.

HENRY. Look. This is not a consultation. I'm just talking to you.

SIDNEY. Forgive me. Old habits die hard. Had you set a precedent?

HENRY. For what?

SIDNEY. Were you unfaithful to her?

HENRY. No. Never.

SIDNEY. Well, there's your problem.

HENRY. What?

SIDNEY. Somebody had to do it. It's usually the man, but ... It's physics. It's library science. The jobs will be filled, the roles will be played. *(Hears something.)* There it is again, but you don't hear it, right? Forget it. Take my wife — I'm not gonna make the joke — Marcia Marie is totally, one thousand percent faithful to me.

HENRY. So do I extrapolate from that that you fuck around?

SIDNEY. In my first marriage, never! Never! I was a paragon.

And my first wife flew on planes to fuck men. She would go vast distances and miss meals to bang a busboy in Council Bluffs. It was my fault. That was my job. And I didn't do it. I indulged in moral luxury. I was a wifely husband. And that ain't the job.

HENRY. What job?

SIDNEY. Manhood.

HENRY. I don't think of manhood as a job.

SIDNEY. It's a job. Done right, it's a tiring job. And women have a lot to do with what that job entails. Sure, women create. The womb. We all acknowledge the womb. But there's another side. And it's not pretty. There's a Hindu deity in India named Kali. The god of destruction. It's a woman. She's got a bloody sword and a appetite for decapitation. In the West, we call her "The Devouring Mother." Creation, destruction. Every woman has these two sides to her, and every man must deal with these two sides. Creation, destruction. You gotta orient a woman in such a way so as to be facing her creative parts. You want the creative parts. The destructive parts … You want those to be facing away. Towards a wall or an enemy or something. Women consume, and they must be directed what to consume, or they may identify you as lunch. You've gotta point them. Like you would a bazooka. Like you would a chainsaw. You don't hold a chainsaw by the chain. Let me pull it together another way. Monogamy is like a forty watt bulb. It works, but it's not enough. Women used to come with goats and textiles. When they got upset, they worked on their textiles and they yelled at their goats. Now they look around, no goats, no textiles. All there is is some schmuck trying to read his newspaper. All right, all right, here it is boiled down to nothing. Don't bet the farm, Henry. That's what I'm trying to say. 'Cause if a woman smells that you're betting the farm on her, you're gonna lose the farm.

HENRY. Maybe you've been at this job too long.

SIDNEY. I didn't learn this on the job. This is home truth.

HENRY. I can't get divorced again.

SIDNEY. You don't have to get divorced. You know my wife Marcia Marie, right?

HENRY. Yeah.

SIDNEY. What do you think of her?

HENRY. She's lovely. She's very nice.

SIDNEY. She's a bag of shit and I have to hold my nose to fuck her.

HENRY. Sidney, we're talking about your wife!

SIDNEY. And the mother of my children.

HENRY. You don't have children.

SIDNEY. Figure of speech.

HENRY. Look, I know you're ... I admire you, Sidney, how you've succeeded at work, the books. But I guess everybody falls down ...

SIDNEY. Fortunately, I don't look to Marcia Marie to pit my peach.

HENRY. How did this become about your marriage?

SIDNEY. I've got another woman for that and she's better than a quart of blood.

HENRY. So you do cheat.

SIDNEY. It's how I passed the bar.

HENRY. There's no way to cheat on the bar.

SIDNEY. I'll choose not to correct you.

HENRY. Even if there is, I wouldn't want it. It wouldn't be right.

SIDNEY. Right? You poor bastard, they've got you by the balls. Right and wrong, that's the corral they use to keep the cows out of the house. A man like you should know better. A man who came from the depths. Henry, we're lawyers. We do not traffic in right and wrong. Come on. That's for chumps. That's for clients.

HENRY. I think Justice exists.

SIDNEY. Good for you. Meet me on Mount Sinai ... we'll do a dance. Answer me this, Moses. What is morality?

HENRY. It's ... I know it when I see it.

SIDNEY. Very good. So do I. It's a franchise. Morality is a chain restaurant. You go there because you know what you're gonna get. One burger. You don't have to think. You don't have to invent a response to the unknown. It's a lot like being dead except you're eating. I had a vision about six months ago. It changed my life. I'd just lost a case. A woman with three kids. One autistic. Her husband stole everything and I couldn't stop him because she was moral and he wasn't. It got me down. I went walking on Jay Street. I looked at the malformed people who actually inhabit this world. And there among them I saw a broken old lady, derelict, starving, blind, ignored, an outcast sitting on the sidewalk. And then,

34

awful, I realized I knew her. Henry, her name was Justice. Everybody just walked around her, pretended she didn't exist. But I saw her. And I resolved, right there, on that street, looking at that lost woman, that I was not going to be her. I was going to get what I need to survive. Irrespective of anybody else's idea of good or right. Two days later, I was down at Borough Hall for a preconference. This clerk was busting my chops and I went out for a breather to the men's room. When outta the ladies room came this girl. And though I didn't know her, I recognized her. Like she was wearing an identifying shackle. She had a limp. It was the sexiest thing I've ever seen.

HENRY. Look, Sidney, I was going to ask you for advice, but you're further out on the peninsula than me.

SIDNEY. You think you can get everything you need from one woman?

HENRY. I don't know. What is everything?

SIDNEY. Good question! What's inside you? What's the scope of Henry? What do you include? Think about it.

HENRY. I am thinking, but what are you doing, man? It sounds to me like you got burned by your first wife, so then you just chose to be a clown or something.

SIDNEY. I am not a clown.

HENRY. I just mean it seems like you're making fun of your own heart. Out of this pain. Like smiling despair or words like that.

SIDNEY. I'm not in despair. I'm not going to kill myself. So what, life is not this pretty thing. I still want it. I want to live. You've seen what passes through this office. You know what's left of love when life is done with it. Bones. We don't have to fear the whirlwind, Henry, we ARE the whirlwind. Now you can go with that, or you can succumb. I've made my choice. I lie. I steal. I cheat. I've chosen life. And I am having a very good time. Marcia Marie and me: It was us. We were living in a TV show. A pilot that wasn't gonna get picked up. I was playing a part. I still play it, but now I know it's just a mask, not the real me at all.

HENRY. But then what are you doing? Why are you still married?

SIDNEY. I'll tell you why! Revenge!

HENRY. For what?

SIDNEY. All that time I towed in the line! Retribution requires a recipient. I need Marcia Marie to lie to, steal from, cheat on! At this point, that's what Marcia Marie is for. She makes it wrong. And wrong is right.

HENRY. Wrong is right.

SIDNEY. Don't repeat me to me. Maybe once in your life you're supposed to do something hard. Some fork in the road. Your soul-saving contribution. But the rest of the time, to call a duck a duck, life is a very dirty party.

HENRY. You're talking too much to be right.

SIDNEY. I'm talking about the thing in all people that you may call evil that has just as much right to expression as anything else in you! I'm talking about not being on your deathbed choking on emotional pus because you didn't once speak. Am I talking about evil? Who cares?! Why did I give you *Crime and Punishment*, Henry? What is conscience? I think it's loneliness. *(He is surprised by tears. Gets them under control.)* Society banishes the man who lives by his own right and wrong. Maybe I do want to be understood. Maybe because you've stumbled on to some kind of hypocrisy in your marriage, you may be open to understanding me. And this thing of mine with this girl. This girl, all the black scum of my long beleaguered heart, she eats. I can't tell you what I've said to her, done to her. The literally most horrible things I could think of! And she comes back for more. She's grateful. God bless her. Yes, I mention God! Because it is like a miracle. We found each other. She's sweet, she's like a kid. She was sad about this pin she lost. I bought her another one. When I give it to her, it will make her day. *(Sidney has taken out an alligator pin. Shows it to Henry.)*

HENRY. Is that an alligator? *(Sidney throws it on his desk.)*

SIDNEY. Some fuckin' reptile. Do you know why I went into matrimonial law?

HENRY. The money?

SIDNEY. Don't be an idiot! It's never about money! YOU MEAN YOU REALLY DON'T HEAR THAT SOUND?! I went into matrimonial law to do for others what I didn't have the courage to do for myself. Sever the conventional bond. I was the most cynical bastard in the world. 'Cause I knew there was no love to be had. All the bitter disappointment of my marriage bed, I turned on the spouses of my clients. That bitch! That bastard! And then I

would go home and kiss that fat pink ass of empty virtue, my wife.
HENRY. But your wife is skinny.
SIDNEY. But I think of her as fat. Despicable! I was a despicable man! I did much harm. But no more. Because now when a man or woman comes in my office and sits here and tells me their dreams have come to nothing, I have something to give them. I have hope.
HENRY. I don't want revenge. I just want my wife.
SIDNEY. Wake up. You got your wife. That's the problem. She's there. *(The phone rings.)* Excuse me. *(He answers the phone.)* What do I pay you for? To not listen? Oh. All right. *(Pause. He turns away and speaks in a voice too low to be heard.)* Yes? Yes, that's right. Why do you want to know? I see. This happened recently? That's terrible. Well no, I don't think I do. Really? But I'm sure I'm not the only one. Of course. Of course. Yeah. Would you mind, I'm in the middle of business. Yeah. *(He hangs up the phone, sits quietly a long moment, peaceful. Then he tears the phone off his desk and throws it violently against the wall.)* God! Jesus! What the fuck!
HENRY. What the hell are you doing?!
SIDNEY. That girl. The girl with the limp. She shot herself. She named me in a note, and then she shot herself. *(Sidney breaks down. Henry comforts him.)* Oh my God, did I do this? Am I responsible?
HENRY. Shh. Shh. Take it easy. Take it easy now.
SIDNEY. And I denied I knew her.
HENRY. That's reflex.
SIDNEY. I gave her the gun!
HENRY. You did?
SIDNEY. It was supposed to protect her. *(We hear a pronounced thump.)* Do you hear it now? Do you hear that thing now?
HENRY. Yeah. What is that? *(Another thump. Horrified, Sidney realizes what it is.)*
SIDNEY. It's her limp! It's Celeste! It's her limp! Jesus, she's coming for me! *(Suddenly, Celeste rises out of the bed in the corner. She is dressed in white. There's a bloodstain. She points at Sidney, who goes white with fear, plastering himself against the opposite wall.)*
CELESTE. Sidney.
SIDNEY. I'm sorry, Celeste! I'm sorry! I'm sorry!

CELESTE. Listen to me.

SIDNEY. That I degraded you to this point of destruction!

CELESTE. I've come to tell you …

SIDNEY. What can I do to make it right?! *(Celeste raises both her hands in supplication.)*

CELESTE. It was not your fault. You were the good part of my life.

SIDNEY. But then why did you do it? Why? *(Celeste wheels on Henry, points an accusing finger, and says:)*

CELESTE. ASK YOUR WIFE! *(Blackout. Something like Charley Musselwhite singing "Baby, Will You Please Help Me" kicks in.*)*

Scene 4

A kitchen table, sun coming in strikes it. Sidney is sitting at the table. Marcia Marie, who wears sexless, neat clothes, is making coffee in a Mr. Coffee machine. She hasn't been happy for a long time. A silence hangs over them.

MARCIA MARIE. I have a confession. I'm disappointed you're home. I like this time for myself.

SIDNEY. Aaa. There was an incident at work.

MARCIA MARIE. What?

SIDNEY. I don't know.

MARCIA MARIE. Did you get fired?

SIDNEY. No. Nobody's gonna fire me, Marcia Marie. I'm a very successful man.

MARCIA MARIE. Did I say different?

SIDNEY. Something.

MARCIA MARIE. I saw a pair of pants today that were very you. I'll tell you where they are. You should go and look at them.

SIDNEY. I can dress myself.

MARCIA MARIE. Did I say different?

SIDNEY. There was a phone call. There was a phone call at work.

---

* See Special Note on Songs and Recordings on copyright page.

MARCIA MARIE. I didn't call you.

SIDNEY. I didn't say you did.

MARCIA MARIE. You can't accuse me of hounding you.

SIDNEY. I'm not.

MARCIA MARIE. I never call except when I have no choice. It's not like the old days when I used to make what you called pointless calls. Distracting you from the great work.

* SIDNEY. Look. This is a tough day for me. Could you lay off?

MARCIA MARIE. Well, this is a tough day for me, too. Maybe you want to go out for a walk till it's the time you usually come home?

SIDNEY. No. If you want somebody to go out, why don't you go out?

MARCIA MARIE. Me? I'm not going anywhere. I'm wiped.

SIDNEY. Wiped from what?

MARCIA MARIE. It's tiring for me when you're here.

SIDNEY. I'm here every morning and every night.

MARCIA MARIE. Not every night.

SIDNEY. Most nights.

MARCIA MARIE. So you can imagine how tired I am.

SIDNEY. Well, this is my home. This is where I can go.

MARCIA MARIE. You have the office.

SIDNEY. Yes, I have an office and then I come home. Those are the two poles of my universe.

MARCIA MARIE. Well, I only have one pole, this is it, and I deserve time alone. You make me nervous.

SIDNEY. You mean just by being alive?

MARCIA MARIE. During the day. In my kitchen. Yes. So I'm making coffee. Do you want some or not?

SIDNEY. Won't coffee make you more nervous?

MARCIA MARIE. At this point, I don't think so. I'm too wiped.

SIDNEY. But from what?!

MARCIA MARIE. You. Your aura. There's only so much of your aura I can take.

SIDNEY. Well, back at ya.

MARCIA MARIE. But I didn't come to your office. You came to my kitchen.

SIDNEY. And did what?

MARCIA MARIE. Don't I deserve anything?

39

SIDNEY. You know, I hate to smack your pinata, but this is my kitchen, too. I paid for this kitchen.
MARCIA MARIE. I paid for this kitchen.
SIDNEY. With what?
MARCIA MARIE. My ass.
SIDNEY. It's our apartment.
MARCIA MARIE. I deserve a room.
SIDNEY. You have your own bathroom.
MARCIA MARIE. Are you trying to drive me into the bathroom now?
SIDNEY. I'm not trying to drive you anywhere. You're trying to drive me out of my own apartment.
MARCIA MARIE. During the day.
SIDNEY. Day, night, what's the difference?
MARCIA MARIE. You don't know the difference between day and night?
SIDNEY. A.M., P.M., shelter is shelter.
MARCIA MARIE. *(To an audience member.)* I'm sorry.
SIDNEY. *(To another audience member.)* Pardon me.
MARCIA MARIE. Pressure.
SIDNEY. Gas Bag.
MARCIA MARIE. I've made peace with the idea of part of you part of the time.
SIDNEY. I've made concessions, too.
MARCIA MARIE. Are you looking for further concessions from me?
SIDNEY. I've come to recognize the need for some form of end of you and beginning of other things, okay?
MARCIA MARIE. Why won't you give me what I want?
SIDNEY. And what is that?
MARCIA MARIE. Space.
SIDNEY. Are there definite limits to the amount of space you need?
MARCIA MARIE. I have none.
SIDNEY. What are we talking about?! What about the ...
MARCIA MARIE. I have nothing. I'm irrelevant. And you remind me. And I can't be reminded all the time. I need breaks.
SIDNEY. To do what?
MARCIA MARIE. Daydream.

40

SIDNEY. About what?

MARCIA MARIE. Big picture? Goods and services. ∧

SIDNEY. You know, you could long and ache and pine for other things besides goods and services.

MARCIA MARIE. Oh but no. You have limited me to dreaming about goods and services, God help me.

SIDNEY. You don't need God. You need a concierge.

MARCIA MARIE. I need my soul.

SIDNEY. Don't look at me.

MARCIA MARIE. I am looking at you. I'm like a check you never endorsed.

SIDNEY. Why should it be up to me to cash you?

MARCIA MARIE. An undeposited check, at a certain point, the bank doesn't honor it anymore. And when the bank doesn't honor you, honey, and you're a check, well, that's bleak.

SIDNEY. Look. You might as well know. I've had a big shock. Never mind about what. But I'm not doing too terrific. I'm having some suicidal ideas.

MARCIA MARIE. I have suicidal ideas.

SIDNEY. Are you gonna vie with me now for the right to be suicidal?

MARCIA MARIE. I'm going to defend myself.

SIDNEY. Against what?

MARCIA MARIE. Your feelings. Your emotional supremacy.

SIDNEY. That's just me talking. I don't wanna rule over you. I want it not to matter what I do.

MARCIA MARIE. Well, it does matter. *(A relenting. He turns away, thinks about it, and finally gives her the small gift box with the alligator pin.)*

SIDNEY. Look. Here.

MARCIA MARIE. What's this?

SIDNEY. A present.

MARCIA MARIE. A pin.

SIDNEY. It's nothing. It's an alligator.

MARCIA MARIE. White enamel. It goes with everything I have.

SIDNEY. Don't make a big thing, put it away.

MARCIA MARIE. It's exquisite.

SIDNEY. It's just costume jewelry. A little doo-dad.

41

MARCIA MARIE. You thought of me.

SIDNEY. I don't know what I was thinking about.

MARCIA MARIE. You were out.

SIDNEY. *(Overlaps.)* Put it away!

MARCIA MARIE. You thought of me.

SIDNEY. *(Overlaps.)* Put it away!

MARCIA MARIE. You went into a store —

SIDNEY. *(Cutting her off.)* Forget it.

MARCIA MARIE. Thank you.

SIDNEY. It's nothing. Forget it. *(Touched by her perception of a tender gesture, she throws herself at Sidney. He tries to get away.)*

MARCIA MARIE. Let's go on a trip. Let's go on a trip.

SIDNEY. *(Overlaps.)* Get your hands off me.

MARCIA MARIE. Please! Please! Please!

SIDNEY. Get your hands off me! Don't make a big thing I said. *(Suddenly, a sexual moment. He grabs her lustfully. Violent grinding. She moans. But he panics, tears free.)* This is why I wanna kill myself. You're a trap! I feel a move of my hand could topple your world.

MARCIA MARIE. That's right. And that's a responsibility.

SIDNEY. Well, I reject that responsibility! In order for me to save you, I have to kill me! And I wanna live! I wanna live. All right. I'm gonna take the steps necessary to stop having these dark ideas. I want a divorce.

MARCIA MARIE. And that's not going to happen. Do you want coffee?

SIDNEY. Can I ask you? What is this? I mean, over time? What are we doing?

MARCIA MARIE. Big picture? We've been killing each other.

SIDNEY. But why? Why would we do that?

MARCIA MARIE. No guts, I guess.

SIDNEY. For what?

MARCIA MARIE. Freedom.

SIDNEY. What would you know about freedom?

MARCIA MARIE. *(She feigns a limp to make her point.)* Oh boy, a slave in her shackles knows about freedom!

SIDNEY. Don't do that. Don't do that.

MARCIA MARIE. Why not?

SIDNEY. Are you superstitious?

42

MARCIA MARIE. Very.

SIDNEY. I didn't know that.

MARCIA MARIE. How else can I explain my life except by thinking that I suffer under a curse of your causing.

SIDNEY. But why me?! What did I do?

MARCIA MARIE. You destroy marriages for a living.

SIDNEY. Whereas you do it gratuitously. You're the inspiration for my work, Marcia Marie. I see myself as saving people. I see myself as goddamn Robin Hood!

MARCIA MARIE. Robin Hood was a glorified thug. As are you.

SIDNEY. I perform a service.

MARCIA MARIE. So do I.

SIDNEY. What?

MARCIA MARIE. I keep you off the market.

SIDNEY. So you're containing me.

MARCIA MARIE. Yes.

SIDNEY. And I'm containing you.

MARCIA MARIE. Containing and invading. You're in my kitchen now. In the daytime.

SIDNEY. Each of us in a smaller and smaller bottle.

MARCIA MARIE. No, you're free.

SIDNEY. But that's not what you said before. That's a contradiction.

MARCIA MARIE. What, are you trying to catch me up?

SIDNEY. I'm trying to understand.

MARCIA MARIE. No.

SIDNEY. You won't let me understand.

MARCIA MARIE. You understand. But I'm not going to help you.

SIDNEY. Why not? *(She goes for the coffee in the pantry.)*

MARCIA MARIE. I have more reasons than there are fish in the sea.

SIDNEY. Name one.

MARCIA MARIE. You know.

SIDNEY. No, I do not know.

MARCIA MARIE. You have been having an affair.

SIDNEY. No, I haven't.

MARCIA MARIE. *(As she pours hot coffee on his hand.)* And you're a liar. *(He yips and jumps away.)*

SIDNEY. I don't wanna do this.

MARCIA MARIE. What?

43

SIDNEY. Actually talk to you.

MARCIA MARIE. No, you don't.

SIDNEY. Or if I do want to talk, this is not the topic. Or even if this is the topic, I can't let you poison the last well I have to drink from. I'm gonna save myself.

MARCIA MARIE. And you think I'm fat.

SIDNEY. What are you talking about?! You're skinny!

MARCIA MARIE. What are YOU talking about? I'm fat! I'm shaking with fat!

SIDNEY. You're a rail, you're a stick, you're practically gaunt!

MARCIA MARIE. But you think of me as fat, don't you!

SIDNEY. Who said that? No!

MARCIA MARIE. Then why don't you fuck me?

SIDNEY. What are you talking about? I do fuck you.

MARCIA MARIE. No, you don't.

SIDNEY. This is surreal.

MARCIA MARIE. You've changed the order of things. That's what men do. They rearrange the truth.

SIDNEY. Whereas you don't even bother with it.

MARCIA MARIE. I am all about the truth.

SIDNEY. No. You are all about cruelty. Every piece of toast in your breadbasket is buttered with cruelty.

MARCIA MARIE. You want some toast? I could make some.

SIDNEY. Are you serious?

MARCIA MARIE. Yeah.

SIDNEY. Jesus. Domesticity.

MARCIA MARIE. You want some toast or not?

SIDNEY. No, I don't want any fucking toast! And you wear those goddamn ugly clothes!

MARCIA MARIE. What's the matter with my clothes?

SIDNEY. They say you're married.

MARCIA MARIE. I am married.

SIDNEY. Those clothes say you fuck by the numbers.

MARCIA MARIE. But I don't fuck by the numbers 'cause you don't fuck me.

SIDNEY. What are you talkin' about? We fuck two-point-eight times a week.

MARCIA MARIE. And you say I'm by the numbers. I don't have

44

sex with you, Sidney. You leave your body, I abandon mine, what's left fucks.

SIDNEY. Well, I hope those faceless homunculi have fun. Whoever they are. *homunculi*

MARCIA MARIE. I have sex with a zombie.

SIDNEY. That's nothing. I have sex with death!

MARCIA MARIE. So you're dead. Lie down.

SIDNEY. I didn't say I was dead, I said I have sex with death.

MARCIA MARIE. Who is she?

SIDNEY. You.

MARCIA MARIE. Easy. Glib. Prick. Just remember. It's not my fault how you feel about who you turned out to be. A flop.

SIDNEY. My life hasn't reached the point of verdict.

MARCIA MARIE. Your life isn't on trial, Sidney. There's nothing to argue about. There's nothing to rule on. You have no case. You're a flop.

SIDNEY. You don't get to say.

MARCIA MARIE. Who knows you better than me?

SIDNEY. You don't know me.

MARCIA MARIE. All I know is you.

SIDNEY. No. The problem is you think I'm you and you detest yourself.

MARCIA MARIE. No, I know who I detest and I know why I detest him. I just can't believe I married him, that's all! I just can't believe I'm here!

SIDNEY. I can't believe I'm here, either! It's implausible that I'm here!

MARCIA MARIE. It's funny!

SIDNEY. Ha. Ha. But why are you here if you don't wanna be here?!

MARCIA MARIE. To make sure you don't get away with it.

SIDNEY. With what?

MARCIA MARIE. No more. Nothing more to say.

SIDNEY. There are people ... There is a woman ... There WAS a woman, who loved me.

MARCIA MARIE. So. Finally. There it is. You admit it.

SIDNEY. Yes. All right. I admit it. I admit the dirty secret that somebody loved me, yes.

*confession
I have to,*

45

MARCIA MARIE. Who?

SIDNEY. Never mind, it's not important. She's gone. She's out of the picture. But without her, the good news is, you become impossible to bear.

MARCIA MARIE. Who was she?

SIDNEY. What do you care?

MARCIA MARIE. Who was she?

SIDNEY. I'm not tellin' you her name.

MARCIA MARIE. Who was she?

SIDNEY. She's gone.

MARCIA MARIE. She ditched you. Well, of course. Sooner or later, they all wake up.

SIDNEY. Not exactly. She's dead.

MARCIA MARIE. She killed herself.

SIDNEY. How'd you know that?

MARCIA MARIE. That's why you were thinking about suicide. Figures. You're so suggestible.

SIDNEY. No, it doesn't figure! It's a tragedy!

MARCIA MARIE. Tragedy is when you fall from a height. Not when a home wrecker hangs herself!

SIDNEY. She didn't hang herself!

MARCIA MARIE. But she was a home wrecker. How did she do it? What did she do? Pills? Jump off a building? No. Takes guts to jump. Or did she shoot herself?

SIDNEY. Are you a fucking witch?

MARCIA MARIE. No. You're the spiritual one. You and your books. You left me nothing but the flesh.

SIDNEY. I'm not talking about this with you anymore.

MARCIA MARIE. So she shot herself. Did she leave a note? Did she name you in the note? Sidney?

SIDNEY. I'm not talking.

MARCIA MARIE. Are you in trouble?

SIDNEY. Potentially. I gave her ... I had given her a gun.

MARCIA MARIE. You stupid ass. Where did you get a gun?

SIDNEY. Some creep. A domestic violence dispute. I don't think it's traceable to me.

MARCIA MARIE. You didn't kill her, did you?

SIDNEY. No.

MARCIA MARIE. Did you?

SIDNEY. No!

MARCIA MARIE. You may need me. The credibility I bring. Or just my brain. I'll do that for you. But what was her name?

SIDNEY. I feel like if I tell you her name ... Maybe this is that fork in the road for me. The one time I'm supposed to do something hard. Or I'll be damned.

MARCIA MARIE. I'm damned. Why shouldn't you be? You stole my soul.

SIDNEY. Go ahead. Frisk me! I don't have it. I don't have your soul. You've ransacked me looking for it. You wrecked me.

MARCIA MARIE. I was lonely.

SIDNEY. You were lonely when I met you.

MARCIA MARIE. Marriage is supposed to end that.

SIDNEY. You were misinformed about the nature of the institution.

MARCIA MARIE. You never gave me a chance. Who was she?

SIDNEY. I should respect this thing she did.

MARCIA MARIE. Blowing her brains out?

SIDNEY. No, something else. Maybe this is that fork in the road for me. I shouldn't betray her name. Maybe you're right. Maybe this marriage is my doing. If it is, I'm sorry. Maybe I just didn't have enough love to conquer all.

MARCIA MARIE. You never gave me a chance. You shut me out.

SIDNEY. No.

MARCIA MARIE. You shut me out. Because your first wife was untrue. You showed up in my life a light-hearted looking man. But your smile and your easiness came out of despair. I didn't understand that.

SIDNEY. But I could've melted. You could've melted me. Like the sun melts the snow.

MARCIA MARIE. I'm just a woman, Sidney. I'm not Spring.

SIDNEY. I've been afraid of you for so long.

MARCIA MARIE. Why would you be scared of me?

SIDNEY. I don't know.

MARCIA MARIE. *(She suddenly explodes.)* Who was she?! Tell me her fucking name!

SIDNEY. No, I won't! It's mine! She loved me! I can't let you touch it!

MARCIA MARIE. You know I'll find out! If I can't have a room, neither can you! I'll just hammer away at you until you give it up! I'll get at it and I'll piss on it!

SIDNEY. I'm leaving you!

MARCIA MARIE. You're not going anywhere! You gave me a pin.

SIDNEY. Forget the pin. Some good's gotta come of this!

MARCIA MARIE. Of what?!

SIDNEY. Her sacrifice.

MARCIA MARIE. You talk about her sacrifice to me? I sold my ass for a kitchen!

SIDNEY. But why did you do that?

MARCIA MARIE. I didn't think I could do better.

SIDNEY. And you don't even have clear title to the kitchen.

MARCIA MARIE. In the eyes of God, this is my kitchen. In the eyes of God, you are my husband.

SIDNEY. You are a materialist. Materialists go mad. They break their possessions to prove that they own them. I'm going to leave you, I'm going to temple, and then I'm going to the police. I won't let you kill anymore. She used to say she could smell murder on me. I knew what she was smelling was you.

MARCIA MARIE. *(She grabs a butcher knife from a drawer.)* You're staying here. With me. Till death. That's the vow! And you're gonna keep it!

SIDNEY. Put down that knife!

MARCIA MARIE. You think you can humiliate me?

SIDNEY. Get a hold of yourself!

MARCIA MARIE. I'll do it! I'll do it! I'll do it! *(She lunges for him three times. He's gotten hold of her knife arm. She kicks at his legs while she struggles. Sidney is crying and terrified.)*

SIDNEY. Stop! Stop! What are you doing?

MARCIA MARIE. You're not going to her!

SIDNEY. She's dead!

MARCIA MARIE. You think I wanted to have this be my life? I. Want. Happiness! *(He gets the knife, She tries to smack him, but she's too weak now. He's panting.)*

SIDNEY. The pursuit of happiness doesn't look like this. *(He throws the knife on the table.)* I'm leaving you. *(He goes to the door, opens it. She picks up the knife. She poises it to stab herself in the*

48

breast.)

MARCIA MARIE. If you walk out that door, I'm shoving this right through my heart. And you can explain two dead women in one day. *(Sidney hesitates, and then gives it up.)*

SIDNEY. Celeste. Her name was Celeste. I bought the pin for her. *(Sidney exits, slamming the door behind him. She stands there with the knife. She yells at the closed door.)*

MARCIA MARIE. I want all the money! All of it! *(She looks at herself in the knife blade and recoils with recognition.)* My mother! *(Blackout.)*

Scene 5

Lights up. Natalie's sitting in Henry's chair, sleeping. Daytime. The door opens. It's Henry. He comes in with a paper deli bag. Natalie starts awake and blurts out.

NATALIE. Tommy?

HENRY. Tommy huh?

NATALIE. Henry.

HENRY. Disappointed? *(She rushes to him.)*

NATALIE. Oh no! What a night I've had!

HENRY. I hear ya.

NATALIE. What's in the bag?

HENRY. Coffee.

NATALIE. I could have made you coffee.

HENRY. You could have closed the front door, but you left it open again.

NATALIE. He came back.

HENRY. Who?

NATALIE. Tommy. He tried to kill me. Look at my neck!

HENRY. I don't see anything. *(She rushes to a mirror, looks at her neck, finds nothing.)*

NATALIE. You don't? I couldn't breathe!

HENRY. Can you breathe now?

NATALIE. Yeah.

HENRY. Just a panic attack.

NATALIE. He was here!

HENRY. I believe you. It's not that.

NATALIE. What have you been doing when you were out?

HENRY. I saw Sidney. We had a talk. You know, I don't want to be Sidney. *(He goes to the CD player.)* Secret music again.

NATALIE. You seem strange.

HENRY. Do I? *(He pulls out three envelopes and throws them on the bed.)* Let's get to it. I put together these three envelopes. You may wanna open this one.

NATALIE. What is it?

HENRY. Twenty-seven hundred dollars.

NATALIE. Thanks.

HENRY. Now you may wanna take that, and you may not. If you take it, you're in debt to me. That's one way to go.

NATALIE. I could pay off my credit cards with this.

HENRY. What about your dead boy Tommy? Gotta pay him back.

NATALIE. I know. I'm just saying.

HENRY. Or you don't have to take the money from me. You could take the second envelope.

NATALIE. What's that one?

HENRY. An application for a joint checking account.

NATALIE. Really?

HENRY. Yeah. Then it would be our money. You could make a withdrawal. You wouldn't be in debt to anybody. You could go that way.

NATALIE. What's in the third envelope?

HENRY. That? That's an action for a divorce.

NATALIE. A divorce?

HENRY. If you choose that envelope, then we divide up our assets, and what you do is not longer my business. So. Natalie. What's it gonna be? Which envelope? *(She looks in the mirror again.)*

NATALIE.   I can't believe there's no mark! It seemed so real! Maybe you're right. Maybe it was just anxiety.

HENRY. What's it gonna be? The divorce, the account, or the cash?

NATALIE. Well, there's a logistical problem, isn't there?

HENRY. How do you mean?

NATALIE. To give the money back.

HENRY. Burn it.

NATALIE. Burn twenty-seven hundred dollars?

HENRY. Yeah.

NATALIE. Would that work?

HENRY. Fuck if I know.

NATALIE. I think you should put it back in the bank.

HENRY. That's not one of these three envelopes. That's us, no joint checking, married, with you in debt to a dead guy. I walked out on that deal last night.

NATALIE. But he's dead. It's too late to pay him back.

HENRY. Tell him that.

NATALIE. Well, I don't want to be out twenty-seven hundred dollars.

HENRY. Okay. So you want a divorce.

NATALIE. I didn't say that!

HENRY. I'm not going to be married like this anymore. I'm not going to be married to a woman who's only half here.

NATALIE. I'm here.

HENRY. Yeah, but you keep forgettin' to close the door.

NATALIE. What's your point?

HENRY. What about Tommy?

NATALIE. He's dead. That's the truth of it.

HENRY. The truth, huh?

NATALIE. That's right.

HENRY. I know you, Natalie. I know what you do in the name of the truth.

NATALIE. What?

HENRY. Serve yourself.

NATALIE. The truth is what it is.

HENRY. What about Justice?

NATALIE. What about it?

HENRY. Which side you on?

NATALIE. My side.

HENRY. You know what I think? There's two kinds of people. The ones that seek, and the ones that hide.

NATALIE. *(Overlaps.)* I'm not hiding from anything.

51

HENRY. But Justice finds you, you know? That's what *Crime and Punishment's* about. You do shit, the clock starts ticking.

NATALIE. Don't talk to me like you're an adult and I'm not. I tell the truth and I pay the price! There should be more people like me.

HENRY. There's plenty of people like you.

NATALIE. Bullshit! Most people lie!

HENRY. You take care of yourself at the expense of everybody else and call it honesty! If that's the truth, then I hate the truth. That truth has no heart. It's ignorant, it's vicious. It's not the human part of people. Now I presented you with three envelopes and I'm askin' you to choose.

NATALIE. You're not asking me! You're a bully! You're the inhuman one! And you know what I say? I say fuck you and fuck your little envelopes. Your little envelopes give me a pain in my ass. You've done nothing always but control me and dominate me with that checking account number and now you're laying out my future like three doors on a game show, and that's inhuman to me! You push me around, Henry. And it's not respectful! I have devoted myself to you and revolved around you and I will not be given choices that I have to choose from. You are a making a crisis when there's nothing wrong!

HENRY. These envelopes, which I cooked up in my fear and my loneliness as a way of dealing with you may be as clumsy and crude as me, but you will not ignore them. You got one foot in and one foot out. You can talk till you're blue. Things can't stay like they are.

NATALIE. You scared me to death with those divorce papers!

HENRY. I'm presentin' you with choices I can live with.

NATALIE. If you can live with divorce, then YOU'VE got one foot out. Your first wife ripped you off and I've been payin' in blood ever since. You've never trusted me!

HENRY. And I was right. You were lying from the getgo.

NATALIE. 'Cause I knew you wouldn't understand.

HENRY. What's to understand? Your wedding dress?

NATALIE. That was before we were married.

HENRY. Well, we're married now.

NATALIE. Are we?

HENRY. I'm here.

NATALIE. Well, I'm here too.

HENRY. No you're not.

NATALIE. Yes I am.

HENRY. What about Tommy?

NATALIE. What about him?

HENRY. You've been carrying a torch for this dead guy.

NATALIE. No!

HENRY. Keepin' his dead ass alive.

NATALIE. Bull!

HENRY. Secret music.

NATALIE. Big deal.

HENRY. Steppin' out on me with fuckin' Frankenstein.

NATALIE. You're nuts!

HENRY. Let him go.

NATALIE. He's dead.

HENRY. He's here.

NATALIE. He's dead.

HENRY. He's here.

NATALIE. *(She hardens.)* I didn't see a ghost. *(A man's arm, Tommy's, smashes through the door and grabs Natalie by the throat. She screams.)* Oh my God!

HENRY. *(Simultaneous.)* Ho! There he is. There's the deadmeat motherfucker himself!

NATALIE. Help!

HENRY. Let her go!

NATALIE. Help!

HENRY. Let her go!

NATALIE. Help!

HENRY. I command you to let her go!

NATALIE. He's not listening to you!

HENRY. Obstinate fucking zombie voodoo motherfucker! Let! Her! Go! *(He pulls her free of the hand. Takes her a few feet away.)*

NATALIE. I'm fine, I'm fine, I'm fine. Let me go! *(Henry lets her go. She flies backward, as if against her will, until Tommy's hand is again around her neck.)* HELP!

HENRY. I can't save you. You don't want to be saved.

NATALIE. Yes I do!

HENRY. Say there's a ghost!

NATALIE. Okay, there's a ghost. *(The ghost releases her.)* What does he want from me?

HENRY. What do you think he wants? He wants the money.

NATALIE. No! *(The ghost force pulls her back into the strangle again. She screams.)*

HENRY. The past isn't done with till you PAY!

NATALIE. I don't want to give him the money! It's mine! I want it to be mine!

HENRY. That's not the same thing.

NATALIE. I want it to be!

HENRY. Wake the fuck up and pay the man his money! *(She pulls herself free of the hand. The door opens. Tommy stands there. We can't see his face. She gets the envelope and hands it over. Tommy takes it.)*

NATALIE. All right. Goddammit. I'll get you your goddamn fucking blood money. Here's your money you cheap bastard. Go back to hell. Now go away! *(She slams the door, and leans against it. To Henry:)* I'm sorry I cheated on you with that guy.

HENRY. I know. You gotta grow up, Natalie.

NATALIE. I know.

HENRY. I can't be going through this once a week. I need help. Life's too hard. It's too lonely.

NATALIE. What do you want?

HENRY. How 'bout love?

NATALIE. Okay.

HENRY. What do you want?

NATALIE. I want a joint checking account.

HENRY. Okay.

NATALIE. That fucking Tommy. Why did I ever have to meet him? And why did he have to be poor?

HENRY. Sit down.

NATALIE. And why couldn't I just take his money and forget it?

HENRY. Because what went on between you and Tommy, that had nothing to do with money. It had to do with love.

NATALIE. I know. I know.

HENRY. It was me. Your marriage to me. That was about money.

NATALIE. Ah, Henry.

HENRY. Stability. You married me for stability.

NATALIE. If I did, is that wrong?

HENRY. Oh baby, it haunts you.

NATALIE. What is marriage?

54

HENRY. I don't know.

NATALIE. Me neither.

HENRY. Wanna find out?

NATALIE. Okay. *(The other door falls with a crash. Celeste's ghost is standing there.)*

CELESTE. Natalie, you lying bitch! Where's my white enamel alligator pin?! Where is it?!

HENRY. Oh yeah, this is the other thing we have to talk about. *(Blackout.)*

End of Play

PROPERTY LIST

Book (SIDNEY, HENRY)
Broom (MARCIA MARIE)
Cell phone (CELESTE)
Coffee, muffin, notebook, pen (CELESTE)
Coffee (NATALIE)
Red beret in purse (CELESTE)
Boom box (HENRY, NATALIE)
Gold medal on chain (HENRY)
Box with joint and lighter (NATALIE)
CD (NATALIE)
Alligator pin in box (SIDNEY)
Phone (SIDNEY)
Mr. Coffee, coffee cups (MARCIA MARIE)
Butcher knife (MARCIA MARIE)
Paper bag with three envelopes (HENRY)

SOUND EFFECTS

Whodunit theme show-type music
Wolf howl
Phone ring
Thump

NEW PLAYS

★ **MONTHS ON END by Craig Pospisil.** In comic scenes, one for each month of the year, we follow the intertwined worlds of a circle of friends and family whose lives are poised between happiness and heartbreak. "...a triumph...these twelve vignettes all form crucial pieces in the eternal puzzle known as human relationships, an area in which the playwright displays an assured knowledge that spans deep sorrow to unbounded happiness." *–Ann Arbor News.* "...rings with emotional truth, humor...[an] endearing contemplation on love...entertaining and satisfying." *–Oakland Press.* [5M, 5W] ISBN: 0-8222-1892-5

★ **GOOD THING by Jessica Goldberg.** Brings us into the households of John and Nancy Roy, forty-something high-school guidance counselors whose marriage has been increasingly on the rocks and Dean and Mary, recent graduates struggling to make their way in life. "...a blend of gritty social drama, poetic humor and unsubtle existential contemplation..." *–Variety.* [3M, 3W] ISBN: 0-8222-1869-0

★ **THE DEAD EYE BOY by Angus MacLachlan.** Having fallen in love at their Narcotics Anonymous meeting, Billy and Shirley-Diane are striving to overcome the past together. But their relationship is complicated by the presence of Sorin, Shirley-Diane's fourteen-year-old son, a damaged reminder of her dark past. "...a grim, insightful portrait of an unmoored family..." *–NY Times.* "MacLachlan's play isn't for the squeamish, but then, tragic stories delivered at such an unrelenting fever pitch rarely are." *–Variety.* [1M, 1W, 1 boy] ISBN: 0-8222-1844-5

★ **[SIC] by Melissa James Gibson.** In adjacent apartments three young, ambitious neighbors come together to discuss, flirt, argue, share their dreams and plan their futures with unequal degrees of deep hopefulness and abject despair. "A work...concerned with the sound and power of language..." *–NY Times.* "...a wonderfully original take on urban friendship and the comedy of manners—a *Design for Living* for our times..." *–NY Observer.* [3M, 2W] ISBN: 0-8222-1872-0

★ **LOOKING FOR NORMAL by Jane Anderson.** Roy and Irma's twenty-five-year marriage is thrown into turmoil when Roy confesses that he is actually a woman trapped in a man's body, forcing the couple to wrestle with the meaning of their marriage and the delicate dynamics of family. "Jane Anderson's bittersweet transgender domestic comedy-drama ...is thoughtful and touching and full of wit and wisdom. A real audience pleaser." *–Hollywood Reporter.* [5M, 4W] ISBN: 0-8222-1857-7

★ **ENDPAPERS by Thomas McCormack.** The regal Joshua Maynard, the old and ailing head of a mid-sized, family-owned book-publishing house in New York City, must name a successor. One faction in the house backs a smart, "pragmatic" manager, the other faction a smart, "sensitive" editor and both factions fear what the other's man could do to this house— and to them. "If Kaufman and Hart had undertaken a comedy about the publishing business, they might have written *Endpapers*...a breathlessly fast, funny, and thoughtful comedy ...keeps you amused, guessing, and often surprised...profound in its empathy for the paradoxes of human nature." *–NY Magazine.* [7M, 4W] ISBN: 0-8222-1908-5

★ **THE PAVILION by Craig Wright.** By turns poetic and comic, romantic and philosophical, this play asks old lovers to face the consequences of difficult choices made long ago. "The script's greatest strength lies in the genuineness of its feeling." *–Houston Chronicle.* "Wright's perceptive, gently witty writing makes this familiar situation fresh and thoroughly involving." *–Philadelphia Inquirer.* [2M, 1W (flexible casting)] ISBN: 0-8222-1898-4

DRAMATISTS PLAY SERVICE, INC.
440 Park Avenue South, New York, NY 10016 212-683-8960 Fax 212-213-1539
postmaster@dramatists.com   www.dramatists.com

NEW PLAYS

★ **BE AGGRESSIVE by Annie Weisman.** Vista Del Sol is paradise, sandy beaches, avocado-lined streets. But for seventeen-year-old cheerleader Laura, everything changes when her mother is killed in a car crash, and she embarks on a journey to the Spirit Institute of the South where she can learn "cheer" with Bible belt intensity. "...filled with lingual gymnastics...stylized rapid-fire dialogue..." –*Variety*. "...a new, exciting, and unique voice in the American theatre..." –*BackStage West*. [1M, 4W, extras] ISBN: 0-8222-1894-1

★ **FOUR by Christopher Shinn.** Four people struggle desperately to connect in this quiet, sophisticated, moving drama. "...smart, broken-hearted...Mr. Shinn has a precocious and forgiving sense of how power shifts in the game of sexual pursuit...He promises to be a playwright to reckon with..." –*NY Times*. "A voice emerges from an American place. It's got humor, sadness and a fresh and touching rhythm that tell of the loneliness and secrets of life...[a] poetic, haunting play." –*NY Post*. [3M, 1W] ISBN: 0-8222-1850-X

★ **WONDER OF THE WORLD by David Lindsay-Abaire.** A madcap picaresque involving Niagara Falls, a lonely tour-boat captain, a pair of bickering private detectives and a husband's dirty little secret. "Exceedingly whimsical and playfully wicked. Winning and genial. A top-drawer production." –*NY Times*. "Full frontal lunacy is on display. A most assuredly fresh and hilarious tragicomedy of marital discord run amok...absolutely hysterical..." –*Variety*. [3M, 4W (doubling)] ISBN: 0-8222-1863-1

★ **QED by Peter Parnell.** Nobel Prize-winning physicist and all-around genius Richard Feynman holds forth with captivating wit and wisdom in this fascinating biographical play that originally starred Alan Alda. "QED is a seductive mix of science, human affections, moral courage, and comic eccentricity. It reflects on, among other things, death, the absence of God, travel to an unexplored country, the pleasures of drumming, and the need to know and understand." –*NY Magazine*. "Its rhythms correspond to the way that people—even geniuses—approach and avoid highly emotional issues, and it portrays Feynman with affection and awe." –*The New Yorker*. [1M, 1W] ISBN: 0-8222-1924-7

★ **UNWRAP YOUR CANDY by Doug Wright.** Alternately chilling and hilarious, this deliciously macabre collection of four bedtime tales for adults is guaranteed to keep you awake for nights on end. "Engaging and intellectually satisfying...a treat to watch." –*NY Times*. "Fiendishly clever. Mordantly funny and chilling. Doug Wright teases, freezes and zaps us." –*Village Voice*. "Four bite-size plays that bite back." –*Variety*. [flexible casting] ISBN: 0-8222-1871-2

★ **FURTHER THAN THE FURTHEST THING by Zinnie Harris.** On a remote island in the middle of the Atlantic secrets are buried. When the outside world comes calling, the islanders find their world blown apart from the inside as well as beyond. "Harris winningly produces an intimate and poetic, as well as political, family saga." –*Independent (London)*. "Harris' enthralling adventure of a play marks a departure from stale, well-furrowed theatrical terrain." –*Evening Standard (London)*. [3M, 2W] ISBN: 0-8222-1874-7

★ **THE DESIGNATED MOURNER by Wallace Shawn.** The story of three people living in a country where what sort of books people like to read and how they choose to amuse themselves becomes both firmly personal and unexpectedly entangled with questions of survival. "This is a playwright who does not just tell you what it is like to be arrested at night by goons or to fall morally apart and become an aimless yet weirdly contented ghost yourself. He has the originality to make you feel it." – *Times (London)*. "A fascinating play with beautiful passages of writing..." –*Variety*. [2M, 1W] ISBN: 0-8222-1848-8

DRAMATISTS PLAY SERVICE, INC.
440 Park Avenue South, New York, NY 10016 212-683-8960 Fax 212-213-1539
postmaster@dramatists.com   www.dramatists.com

NEW PLAYS

★ **SHEL'S SHORTS by Shel Silverstein.** Lauded poet, songwriter and author of children's books, the incomparable Shel Silverstein's short plays are deeply infused with the same wicked sense of humor that made him famous. "...[a] childlike honesty and twisted sense of humor." *–Boston Herald.* "...terse dialogue and an absurdity laced with a tang of dread give [*Shel's Shorts*] more than a trace of Samuel Beckett's comic existentialism." *–Boston Phoenix.* [flexible casting] ISBN: 0-8222-1897-6

★ **AN ADULT EVENING OF SHEL SILVERSTEIN by Shel Silverstein.** Welcome to the darkly comic world of Shel Silverstein, a world where nothing is as it seems and where the most innocent conversation can turn menacing in an instant. These ten imaginative plays vary widely in content, but the style is unmistakable. "...[*An Adult Evening*] shows off Silverstein's virtuosic gift for wordplay...[and] sends the audience out...with a clear appreciation of human nature as perverse and laughable." *–NY Times.* [flexible casting] ISBN: 0-8222-1873-9

★ **WHERE'S MY MONEY? by John Patrick Shanley.** A caustic and sardonic vivisection of the institution of marriage, laced with the author's inimitable razor-sharp wit. "...Shanley's gift for acid-laced one-liners and emotionally tumescent exchanges is certainly potent..." *–Variety.* "...lively, smart, occasionally scary and rich in reverse wisdom." *–NY Times.* [3M, 3W] ISBN: 0-8222-1865-8

★ **A FEW STOUT INDIVIDUALS by John Guare.** A wonderfully screwy comedy-drama that figures Ulysses S. Grant in the throes of writing his memoirs, surrounded by a cast of fantastical characters, including the Emperor and Empress of Japan, the opera star Adelina Patti and Mark Twain. "Guare's smarts, passion and creativity skyrocket to awesome heights..." *–Star Ledger.* "...precisely the kind of good new play that you might call an everyday miracle...every minute of it is fresh and newly alive..." *–Village Voice.* [10M, 3W] ISBN: 0-8222-1907-7

★ **BREATH, BOOM by Kia Corthron.** A look at fourteen years in the life of Prix, a Bronx native, from her ruthless girl-gang leadership at sixteen through her coming to maturity at thirty. "...vivid world, believable and eye-opening, a place worthy of a dramatic visit, where no one would want to live but many have to." *–NY Times.* "...rich with humor, terse vernacular strength and gritty detail..." *–Variety.* [1M, 9W] ISBN: 0-8222-1849-6

★ **THE LATE HENRY MOSS by Sam Shepard.** Two antagonistic brothers, Ray and Earl, are brought together after their father, Henry Moss, is found dead in his seedy New Mexico home in this classic Shepard tale. "...His singular gift has been for building mysteries out of the ordinary ingredients of American family life..." *–NY Times.* "...rich moments ...Shepard finds gold." *–LA Times.* [7M, 1W] ISBN: 0-8222-1858-5

★ **THE CARPETBAGGER'S CHILDREN by Horton Foote.** One family's history spanning from the Civil War to WWII is recounted by three sisters in evocative, intertwining monologues. "...bittersweet music—[a] rhapsody of ambivalence...in its modest, garrulous way...theatrically daring." *–The New Yorker.* [3W] ISBN: 0-8222-1843-7

★ **THE NINA VARIATIONS by Steven Dietz.** In this funny, fierce and heartbreaking homage to *The Seagull*, Dietz puts Chekhov's star-crossed lovers in a room and doesn't let them out. "A perfect little jewel of a play..." *–Shepherdstown Chronicle.* "...a delightful revelation of a writer at play; and also an odd, haunting, moving theater piece of lingering beauty." *–Eastside Journal (Seattle).* [1M, 1W (flexible casting)] ISBN: 0-8222-1891-7

DRAMATISTS PLAY SERVICE, INC.
440 Park Avenue South, New York, NY 10016 212-683-8960 Fax 212-213-1539
postmaster@dramatists.com www.dramatists.com